CHRIST

Will You Marry Me?

How well do you know your coming Bridegroom?

Will You Marry Me?
Trilogy Christian Publishers A Wholly Owned Subsidiary of Trinity Broadcasting Network
2442 Michelle Drive Tustin, CA 92780
Copyright © 2024 by Christa Griffin

All Scripture quotations are taken from the New King James Version®. Copyright © 1982 by Thomas Nelson. Used by permission. All rights reserved.

No part of this book may be reproduced, stored in a retrieval system, or transmitted by any means without written permission from the author. All rights reserved. Printed in the USA.
Rights Department, 2442 Michelle Drive, Tustin, CA 92780.
Trilogy Christian Publishing/TBN and colophon are trademarks of Trinity Broadcasting Network.
For information about special discounts for bulk purchases, please contact Trilogy Christian Publishing.
Trilogy Disclaimer: The views and content expressed in this book are those of the author and may not necessarily reflect the views and doctrine of Trilogy Christian Publishing or the Trinity Broadcasting Network.
Manufactured in the United States of America
10 9 8 7 6 5 4 3 2 1
Library of Congress Cataloging-in-Publication Data is available.
ISBN: 979-8-89333-835-5
E-ISBN: 979-8-89333-836-2

Dedication

This book is dedicated to my earthly Prince Charming, my husband, Tim. Tim, you have been my encourager through every step of the publication of this book. You have encouraged me and showed your pride in me for following my dream of getting these ideas in print. I love you, and I thank God for blessing me with you as my husband. Thank you for believing in me.

Table of Contents

Introduction 9

Chapter 1: Our Coming Bridegroom,
the Prince of Peace 13

Chapter 2: Spending Time with Him 21

Chapter 3: Communication with Him. 31

Chapter 4: Reading His Messages 41

Chapter 5: Getting to Know All About Him 51

About the Author. 57

Introduction

We see in so many of our stories and fairy tales how they talk about a prince coming in on His white horse to save the day and take the princess away to his castle in the sky. While more modern times have seen that women are not so much the damsel in distress we once were depicted to be, we can see where some of these stories may have gotten their inspiration from. What if these ideas come from the Prince of Peace Himself, Jesus? This may seem a little farfetched or "out there" for some ways of thinking, but the Bible does talk of Jesus coming back for His Bride, the Church, one day. And on a white horse, no less . . .

What if we took this idea and looked at it from a new point of view? We hear all the time that we, who are saved, are part of the Bride of Christ. While taking this to heart, can we look at Jesus as our betrothed? If so, can we take a look at how we interact with our betrothed? I believe we can. I believe we can absolutely look at Jesus as our betrothed, the coming Prince of Peace and Bridegroom. And as we continue with this train of thought in this book, we can look at the possibility of seeing Jesus as our betrothed and coming Bridegroom and learn how we can build a relationship with Him, to prepare ourselves for His coming and for our coming wedding day.

"Will You Marry Me?"

—Prince Charming

Chapter 1

Our Coming Bridegroom, the Prince of Peace

Every girl has heard the old phrase, "waiting for Prince Charming to come riding in on his white horse and take her to live in his castle in the sky," but where does this image come from? This image is driven home to us even in our own fairy tales. Snow White, for instance, sings that one day her prince will come to take her away. Taylor Swift had a number-one hit several years ago with her song "White Horse." In Walt Disney's *Snow White*, the main character sings that someday her prince will come, and then at the end of the movie we see her prince come—on a white horse, no less—and take her away to his castle. Hmm, now, where have we seen this scenario play out before? So many of our fairy tales, and even our ideas of chivalry, play out in this vision of a brave prince or a knight in shining armor on a great white steed coming in and saving the day. Have we ever wondered where the idea of a knight on a white charger might have come from? Have we ever considered that maybe this idea comes from somewhere we did not realize? Perhaps this idea comes from the greatest love story ever told. Just maybe it comes from the Prince of Peace Himself, our Bridegroom, Jesus Christ.

In Revelation 19:7, John tells us about the Marriage Supper of the Lamb. The Bride of Christ is clothed in fine linen, clean and white. The Bride is made up of the redeemed, which includes you and me, saved believers who were bought with the precious blood of Jesus. Therefore, we can deduce that once we are saved and give our lives to Christ, we become part of His Bride.

In the book of Revelation, John also talks about Christ coming back to earth on His white horse to get His bride and right all the wrongs of earth, setting all things to right (Revelation 19:11–16). Sound familiar? Maybe what we have been taught in our fairy tales and in those medieval stores of chivalry is closer to reality than we think. Perhaps instead of looking to mortal man for our Prince Charming, we should be looking to our eternal Prince Charming instead. Because, let's face it, mortal men are just men, but Jesus is the *King*! That is not to say we cannot find a prince among mortal man—I myself have, indeed, found a prince among the paupers—but if we look at the book of Revelation and continue with this line of thinking, we will soon see that our relationship with our coming Prince Charming is one of much more importance than we previously may have thought.

I am about to take you down a line of thinking that you may never have thought about before. This may be a modern spin on the old-time fairy tale, but just stay with me and my line of thinking. I promise this will come into focus soon. If we are part of the Bride of Christ once we are saved, then can we not say that we are essentially betrothed to Him at this point? Or, the more modern term would be "engaged." We are essentially engaged to our coming Bridegroom in heaven. Are you still with me? I know this is a new way to think of this, and please know I am not talking about any type of romantic love here—but a pure *agape* love that we have for our Savior and that He has for us.

Our relationship with Jesus involves much more than just receiving Him as our Savior and Lord; we are being prepared to be His Bride. You have to really understand what that means. We are being prepared for a wedding one day, when we will marry our coming Bridegroom, our Prince of Peace, who will soon be coming on a white horse and taking us to His castle in the sky. I know most of us have probably never looked at Jesus' coming in this way, but every time I watch those movies and I see the end, when the prince is standing there and it zooms in on the castle in the clouds, I get glory bumps. That is a picture of what we will one day see. Our Bridegroom will be taking us home to his castle in the sky.

Let's continue to build on this idea of Jesus as our coming Bridegroom, as we have all been taught, that as believers, we are part of the "Bride of Christ." I am not sure if we as believers really understand the concept of this, as experiencing an actual wedding that will occur in the heavens, but it most assuredly is. We are being prepared for this wedding and to be part of His Bride. We have been taught to make ourselves ready, for "our Bridegroom cometh," to be ready as a chaste virgin, dressed in fine linen (Revelation 19:9–10).

If it is true that our betrothed, or "fiancé," if you will, is coming on His white horse to take us away to His castle in the sky, then I want to put this main idea to you, that you have a *heavenly fiancé*. Once you are saved and become part of the Bride of Christ, you are essentially engaged to Him. Now, this puts our relationship with Jesus in a whole new light! In this relationship, then, how do we treat this fiancé? If we have an earthly fiancé, how does this earthly relationship differ from how we treat our heavenly relationship with Jesus? Do we talk to him or her only when we need something? Do we go to see him or her only once a week, or whenever we "feel like it"? Do we choose not to read any love letters they may send us? How much more do we need to build that heavenly relationship than we do an earthly one?

Granted, we are promised that Christ will never "break off" our "engagement" with Him. If we mess up, if we cheat on Him with other things, or make other things more important than Him, Jesus will always be there. We have the promise that once He has us, He will never let us go. John 10:27–30 assures us that no one is strong enough to snatch us out of His hand. He will always forgive us and bring us back into the fold. He is *always* there. How wonderful it is to have a man who has promised to *always* be there. He will never forsake you nor forget you. You could do the most horrific thing imaginable, and He will always take you back. He will clean you up and love you just as much as He did before.

This is shown in the book of Hosea. The tale of Hosea and Gomer is a sad story through which God shows us how much He loves us. God told Hosea to marry a prostitute named Gomer. Hosea did so, and they had some children together, but then she went back to the brothel. We see in Hosea chapter 3 that Gomer had gone back to the brothel and Hosea went in and had to pay for her time. He paid fifteen shekels of silver and one and a half homers of barley just to talk to his wife and bring her back home. This may seem like a very odd story to be included in the Bible, but through it, God is showing us what He does with us. We can turn away from God and do the most awful things. But He paid a price for us, and He cleans us back up and brings us home. He still loves us. God uses this story to paint a picture for us to see how His love works. To most of us, leaving our family to be a prostitute would be about the worst thing we could do to our family members—to choose a lifestyle like this over a family who loves us and takes care of us. But this is the picture God shows to help us see what it's like for Him when we turn from Him. He takes us back time after time.

Also, He will never leave you. So many of us have been left or hurt by earthly relationships. We have been heartbroken so many times by men who have left us or hurt us, but Jesus gives us the promise that He will never leave us nor forsake us (Hebrews 13:5). He is truly our Knight in shining armor, who will fight for us and never leave us.

But just like any earthly relationship, we still need to cultivate this heavenly relationship, as well. You wouldn't want to marry someone you don't know, and neither does Christ. We have to learn how to build that relationship, just like we would with someone we are dating or married to here on earth. When you think about building a relationship with your significant other, how did you start out? What did you do to build that acquaintance into a meaningful relationship? How did you fall in love with that person and decide you wanted to spend your life with them? And remember, here on earth, we vow "'til death do us part." Well, in heaven there will be no death, so our marriage to Christ will be for eternity. How much more do we need to build a relationship with Jesus? We will be with Him much longer than any other relationship we may experience while here on the earth.

So, what do we do, or how do we cultivate this relationship? We start off the same way we do any earthly relationship: We spend time with that person, we usually talk to them on the phone or text multiple times a day, and we always make sure we read and answer all their emails or letters.

In the coming chapters, we will take an in-depth look at each of these points. We will see how we can cultivate a relationship with Christ that will help us to know Him better and move us closer to Him than ever before in our Christian walk. We will look at ways we can spend time with Him, talk to Him, and read His ultimate love letter to us. My hope is that through this book, you will come to see your relationship with your coming "Prince Charming" to be more important than ever. You will be willing to spend a little more time getting to know the

Will You Marry Me?

King of kings in a way you never have before, to help both of you know each other better and not be looking at marrying a stranger when that day comes.

Chapter 2

Spending Time with Him

We established in the previous chapter a line of thinking in which we are essentially engaged to Jesus, as we are part of His Bride. Okay, so what is next? We have met this amazing Man and given our heart to Him. We have asked Him to come into our hearts, save us from our sins, and create a new life within us. What do we do next?

That is a question that many new Christians have: *I have accepted Jesus as my Savior, now what? How do I begin to live this new life? How do I start a relationship with this Man whom I have given my heart to and made my Savior?* Well, the answer is the same as it is for any other relationship we may have. You spend time with Him daily. You get to know Him in a deeper and more meaningful way. Now, you may ask, how do you spend time with

Christ? I cannot be with Him physically and spend time with Him. No, we are not able to see Him or be with Him in the same way we are with other people, but we are able to be with Him spiritually. When we are saved, the Holy Spirit comes to live inside of us (Ephesians 1:13), so when we say we are spending time with Jesus, we are talking about spending time in His Word, letting His Word speak to us through the Holy Spirit and communing with Him through this. As we have our daily quiet time with Jesus and create a set time and place for us to meet with Him, we can grow to understand Him in a much deeper understanding and knowledge of who He is and how He communicates with us through His Word. Christ is the Living Word. John 1 talks about how: "In the beginning was the Word, and the Word was with God, and the Word was God." (John 1:1). John is talking about Jesus here and how He is the Word of God. So, if we spend time reading His Word, it just stands to reason we will grow closer to the One who is the Word.

Another way we spend time with Christ is by attending church regularly. If you want to get really "modern thinking" with this, you can look at it this way. Our daily quiet time in God's Word would be like us talking to someone via the phone or text. When we are dating our earthly fiancé or significant other, we talk to them via the phone or text every day. Then we might see them in person a couple times a week. We get dressed up nice and possibly go out to see them or something like that. Well, that is a way to look at this relationship with Christ, as well. Spending time in God's Word talking to Him daily is like texting or talking on the phone to our earthly fiancé each day. Then when you get dressed nice and all cleaned up to see them in person each week, that would be the equivalent of going to church. We can start to see why church attendance is important. It is that time when we show the world, *This is my Savior, and I am proud to be with Him.*

This also gives you the opportunity to share with others what you have learned about your Savior this week. Coming together with other believers and sharing what you learned about Jesus, as well as learning what they experienced, is the best part of going to church. It says in Hebrews 10:25 that we are not to forsake the gathering together of believers. Why do you think this is? This is because God knows we need to be around other people who are going through the same experiences we are. We need that interaction with other believers to gain strength from them and to have the connection with other people whom we can talk to about our relationship with Christ and have them understand what we are going through.

In an earthly relationship, if you went all week and only spent time with your fiancé once a week or once a month or just whenever you felt like it, that relationship would most likely fall apart before it got started. This same principle is true of our relationship with Christ. We cannot say we have a close relationship with Christ if we only spend time with Him when we feel like it, or when we think about it, or when we feel guilty about it.

You have to work on your earthly relationships; you also must work on your heavenly relationship, as well. Of course, those of us who have a wonderful earthly relationship with our husbands/boyfriends may find that working on that earthly relationship is not considered "work," because you love that person and want to be with them and do anything you can for them. This is how our relationship with Christ should be.

Whom should we love more and want to please more than the one Man who loved us so much that He gave His life for us, enduring the cross of Calvary for us? How much more can He love us than any earthly love could ever be? Mind you, I am not speaking of a romantic love here. The love we may feel for our earthly partner is something different from the love we have for Christ and that He has for us. I am speaking of an even more pure love. The Bible calls this *agape* love. It is the term used to explain the love God has for His people and the love Christ has for the Church. It is a pure love, a more powerful love than any of us could ever comprehend. It is the love of God.

How many of us know anyone, besides maybe our parents, who would actually die for us because they loved us so much? Christ loves us this much and more. Christ died for us two thousand years ago. He had never met us or talked to us, yet He did this for us. He even died for the men who nailed Him to the very cross on which He would die. Can any of us comprehend this kind of *agape* love? And yet, we still have a hard time finding time to be with Him. Just because He is not visible to us, so that we cannot put our arms around Him and hug Him for what He has done for us, that does not mean we cannot show our love for Him in other ways. We as women know about wanting to be shown we are loved in more than physical ways. We want our partners to show us they love us in ways other than physically, and so does Christ. When we want our partners to show us they love us in other ways, we usually want them to spend time with us. Go on a date with us. We want to know they think we are special and that they want to be with us more than they want to be with anyone else. These are things that let us know they love us. Think of it this way: When we go to church, we can look at it as if we are getting ready to go on a date with Jesus. We are going to take some time out of our busy life to spend time with the One who loves us more than anyone in the world. We get dressed up in our best outfit (whatever that may be for you is fine, for Jesus does not care about fashion). We get all fixed up and looking nice, and then we go and we have a gathering of our best friends and family to spend time with our coming Prince. How long has it been since you went on a date with Jesus? How many times have you stood Him up in the last month? He is always there, waiting on you to show up, and He is disappointed when you are not there and He is stood up yet again. If we really looked at the way we treat Jesus, would we be ashamed of how we treat Him? He wants to know that we love Him. He wants us to want to spend time with Him.

And this brings us to the second point in this section: we have to *want* to spend time with Him. Look at it in this light: if you knew that your husband only spent time with you because he knew it was the best way to get something out of you that he wanted or because he *had* to, how would that make you feel? You wouldn't feel very loved, would you? You would feel pretty upset that he didn't really love you the way he said, because if he did, it would make him happy just to be with you. This is the very way we treat Christ when we say, "Oh, I'm not going to church today. I just don't feel like it." Or. "I don't feel like reading my Bible today, I'm too tired." Imagine how you would feel if your husband told you that. "Oh, I don't want to spend time with you tonight. I'm just too tired." Now, maybe that would be alright if he'd had a bad day or something, but if it happened every day for several days or months on end? I don't believe that would go over too well. I believe you would be very upset by this, as you would have every right to be.

You will come to discover that the more time you spend with Christ in His Word, learning more about Him, the more you will love Him. I am sure not many of us have experienced love at first sight. Maybe lust at first sight, but not love. No beam of light shined down with angels singing, "There he is . . ." My husband would like to think that is what happened, but it did not. You spent time with your boyfriend; you went on dates, had romantic dinners, went to the movies, and did things together you had in common, and over the course of time, you fell in love. If this is the way it works for people in an earthly relationship, why is it we can't understand that the same concept runs true in our heavenly relationship with Christ? I find that when I am really into studying His Word, spending time with Him daily, that is when I grow closer to Him and grow to love Him more.

We are to love Christ more than we love any other thing in this world. He is to be first in our lives, which means that we are to put Him before anyone else. That includes yourself, your husband/boyfriend, and your children. Yes, shocking, I know, but we are to put Christ before everyone else. I know in our modern society, we are putting those children before everything else, but that is not the way God intended. God is first, spouse is second, and those children are third. I know this is controversial in our time, but it is the way God designed the family to work. Christ is to be FIRST! How do we show Christ He is first in our lives? By doing His will and obeying Him, by going to church, and by reading and studying His Word to learn more about Him.

So, now we understand that we have to cultivate a relationship with our heavenly Fiancé. We can now see why spending that time with Christ on a daily basis is so very important to our Christian walk. The more time we spend with Christ and the more we love Him, the more we are going to want others to experience the same thing we have with Him.

When you fell in love with your husband, you wanted to introduce him to everyone you knew, because you wanted everyone to meet this wonderful person you had just fallen in love with. It will be the same with Christ. The more you learn to love Him, the more you will want others to meet this most wonderful Person you have just fallen in love with. You will become a warrior in soul-winning for Christ, because you will want to tell everyone you know about this most wonderful, amazing Man you have just had the privilege to get to know and fall in love with. You will not let a conversation go by in which you do not say, "Let me tell you what Jesus spoke to me today. Let me tell you about the time I spent with Jesus this morning." Just like we tell our friends and neighbors about the things we experience in our earthly relationships, we will want to share the experiences we have had that day in our heavenly relationship, as well.

When most of us started dating our husbands, our friends and family got tired of hearing about them most likely. How wonderful would it be if those same friends and family members got tired of hearing about Jesus? About how we are so excited for our relationship with our coming Bridegroom? If we will spend time with Jesus, we will get to that point with Him, just like we did with our husbands before. We will have a desire to share Him with everyone we meet and want them to know Him and love Him just as much as we do. We will build that relationship with Jesus just like we built our relationship with our spouse. You will see that you will fall more in love with Jesus as that relationship builds, and you will be excited at the thought of meeting your Prince one day.

Chapter 3

Communication with Him

We have now determined how we are to spend time with Christ. We must now consider our second point: communication with Him daily. When we are in an earthly relationship, we make sure that we talk with our "other half" at least once a day. More than likely, with cell phones and texting these days, there is hardly an hour or so that goes by that we don't somehow communicate with our partners. First Thessalonians 5:17 says that we are to "pray without ceasing," which simply means we need to talk to Him without stopping. All prayer is, is talking to God. God doesn't need a phone number or a text in order to hear you. His direct line is always open. You will never get a busy signal or a dropped call with Him. You don't have to make a special "date" with Him. He is there at 3 a.m. when you can't sleep because something is bothering you, and He is there at 3 p.m. when you are at work and just can't take it anymore. He is always there for you, whenever and however you need Him.

He wants to know you personally. He wants you to talk to Him just like you do to your fiancé on earth. You may say, "Well, He already knows everything, so why does He want me to tell Him this?" Because He wants that intimacy with you. He wants to know you will come to Him with your needs, problems, and complaints. It's just like a parent and child: the parent knows the child wants something or did something wrong, but the parent wants that child to come to them and ask them or tell them they did something wrong on their own. That is how trust is built. It's just the same with Christ: He wants you to talk to Him. Confide in Him, tell Him about the nut who pulled out in front of you in the car today, tell Him about how your day went, praise Him for not letting you hit that nut who pulled out in front of you today or say any words He would not approve of when it happened. Ask Him to forgive you for what you said or thought about that nut. Also, if you did say those words or have those thoughts, tell Him you're sorry. Just talk to Him. We, as women, what is our number-one complaint about men? Communication! "He never listens to me." Well, here is a Man who wants you to talk His ears off and who will listen to you! What a MAN!

Jesus wants that relationship with you, and your soul actually cries out for that relationship with Him. Once we are saved and the Holy Spirit comes to live inside us, our spirit cries out to have fellowship with God. In Ephesians 4:30, Paul tells us not to grieve the Holy Spirit. Our spirit will become grieved if we do not spend time with God and it does not get fed properly. Our own spirit cries out to have this personal relationship with Christ. When the Holy Spirit becomes grieved in our lives, it makes it more difficult for Him to work on our behalf. We become less receptive to His direction in our lives. It makes it harder for us to hear from God and even harder for us to live the way He would have us to live. It is almost like we turn a deaf ear or silence the Spirit in our lives. We are no longer tender to His guidance, and we are more open to not following His will for our lives. This is why it is extremely important to be sure we are communicating with God every day. We must ensure that we are sensitive to His leadership in our lives. We must make sure that we are living our lives in His will. It keeps us from making so many mistakes. It keeps us from so much heartache. If we are in tune with Him and following His will, we will never have to worry that we are on the wrong path and have to make a hard choice to correct that path.

Imagine if you can, the God of the universe, the One who spoke all things into being, wants to take time out of His schedule to sit down one-on-one with you and talk to you. He will let everything else fade away, and He will stay one-on-one with you. Now, I don't know *any* earthly man who can do that! Our husbands will make time for us, but how many times are we in the middle of talking about something and they are watching TV? How many times have we said, "Are you listening to me?" With Christ, we need never do that. We have His undivided attention whenever we want it.

Picture this scenario in your mind: You need to talk to Him, so you bow your head to pray or you just do it silently in your head (if you are driving, you don't need to bow your head, that nut is still out there!). Somewhere up in heaven, your "Fiancé" says, "Wait just a minute, Susie needs me, I'll be right back," and He comes to listen to you and let you know that He loves you and is there for you, no matter what. If that picture does not give you glory bumps, I don't know what will! That is a picture *any* woman can love! He will stop and talk just to you whenever you need Him to. Now, we all know that Christ is omnipresent, so He can be anywhere, anytime. But if we are to put this in layman's terms and try to see this as a true relationship, I believe we can look at it in these terms and see just how special each and every one of us is to Him. While Jesus is the ultimate multitasker, we can look at it in this way, that when we need Him, He is always there for us.

The next point we are going to look at is listening to Him. In any relationship, the conversation does not go very far if only one person is talking all the time. We have to have an open line of communication that works both ways. Just like in our earthly relationships, if we do not listen to our partner, we cannot know how they are feeling or what they need from us. If we are only concerned with talking and not listening, the relationship will not flourish. The other person feels like we do not hear them, and that is when the issues begin. If you will take the time to listen, Jesus will answer you. He not only listens to all our complaints without interrupting us, but if we will get in His Word and learn to listen, He will answer us and tell us what we need to do. You can't get any better advice than that.

How do we listen to Him? By being quiet and just listening. Sometimes when we pray we need to be quiet and just listen. Some would call this meditation. While you are reading your Bible or praying, just sit and think about what you just read or what you just talked to Him about. I think sometimes teachers or preachers say, "Just listen," and they expect people to know what that means. It truly is as easy as just sitting in a quiet place or listening to some praise music and being open to what the Spirit is saying. We just need to be quiet and concentrate on Him and on the Word we were reading or the song to which we are listening. Several scriptures deal with listening to

God and what He is trying to communicate with us. In the Old Testament, we see God talking directly to people. Moses and the burning bush is a great example of this. In the gospels of the New Testament, Jesus was here—God with us. The disciples had Him there to ask Him their questions. In the book of Acts, we see the Holy Spirit come on the scene. As I stated before, as Christians, we have the Holy Spirit living inside us, so we have Him with us at all times. With that being the case, you would think it would be easier for us to hear from God, but it seems we get so busy with the worldly noise that we drown out what the Holy Spirit is trying to tell us. This is why it is so important to have that quiet time with Him, so that we are able to quiet the noise and be able to hear what God is trying to tell us. As I painted the picture for you before, of Jesus taking time out to be with us one-on-one and listen to us, being there for us, we need to do the same with Him. We need to make time to be one-on-one with Him, so we can be sure to hear what He is trying to tell us. We must concentrate on what He may be trying to tell us. He will talk if we will listen.

God will speak to us all in different ways, as well. Not only does He speak in those quiet, one-on-one times, but He will also speak to us in other ways. Most of the time with me it is a feeling or an idea I will get. I will ask God to help me with a certain situation, and then an idea or something will just come to me—something I would never have thought to do on my own. That is when I know it was from God. It will surprise you sometimes how this works. Sometimes you might hear a lyric in a song, and you will think, "Okay, God, I hear you." Most of the time that is how it works with me. I will just have the "okay" or "aha" moment, when God just seems to say, "This is what I meant by that," and I will say, "Okay, I get it," usually while looking at the ceiling. I can be sitting in church listening to the sermon, and I will get an idea or have something come to my mind. I usually have a pen and paper ready to write it down since it has happened so often. Actually, the idea for this book happened that way. I was sitting in church listening to my husband preach, and the idea for this book just started to spill out on the paper as I was writing. At the time, I remember thinking it was a crazy idea, that Jesus is my Fiancé . . . people would think I was nuts. But as I started to think on it, I came to see it was an idea the Lord wanted me to share. I am not telling you not to pay attention to the sermon or your pastor, but if the Lord starts to speak to you through that sermon, you may want to listen to Him. I'm sure your pastor will understand.

Other times it might be that a person comes up to you and tells you something or asks you to do something. That could let you know, "Okay, God, I get it." It may be different for some you. I have yet to have a beam of light just come down and illuminate something with an angel chorus singing to show me that is what I am to do. It is in the small voice that you can hear, but only if you are really listening and in tune with Him. When I met my husband, there was no illuminating light from heaven that shone around him with angels singing. He might like to think that is what happened, but it's not. It was in the little things that I knew I loved him and that he was the one God had picked for me. It's the same way in other things as well. Be in tune to recognize when these things happen. Sometimes we may have something happen, and if we are not in tune with God, we might miss what He is trying to tell us. You just have to be willing to listen and be patient enough to wait until you hear from Him.

That is the hardest part—the part that requires patience. We live in a "get 'er done" society. We want our food microwaved, our messages texted, our letters emailed, and our questions answered when we ask them. But we have to be willing to do things in God's time. His timing is perfect, and He knows what we need when we need it. I cannot count how many times I have wondered why something was taking so long, but when it finally happened, I understood the reason. In whatever situation you may be facing, know that God wants what is best for you, and His timing is perfect. The hardest part is the waiting. We look around, and others seem to be getting exactly what they ask for when they ask for it. We have to remember that each of us is on a different path, and

God knows what is best for us. He only ever wants what is best for us. He never wishes any harm to come to us. Trust in that and in His timing. If we will wait on God's timing and not try to force things to happen, we will be so much better for it. As women, we are fixers. We kiss the boo-boos, and we mend the hearts. We keep everything running, and we fix the problems. We are the problem-solvers for our homes many times. It is very hard for us to have a problem that we cannot fix. It is even harder for us to wait for someone else to fix it. That is why we have the honey-do list, and men do not. Isaiah 40:31 says for us to wait on the Lord and He will renew our strength. Psalm 27:14 says, "Wait on the Lord; be of good courage, and He shall strengthen your heart; wait, I say, on the Lord." It's all in His will and His timing.

So, in conclusion, we have learned that we have to learn to "talk" to our heavenly Fiancé. He wants to talk to us and have that one-on-one, personal time with us. All we have to do to give Him that is to just take a few moments each day and let Him know how much He means to us and how thankful we are to Him for all He has done for us. It's just as simple as telling Him when you get up in the morning how much you love Him and thank Him for blessing you with another wonderful day. We as women love to talk with our significant others. We love getting to know them and their feelings on things. We love it when they sit and talk with us and show interest in our wants and desires. Christ wants to know those things about us, as well. He desires to know us and have us bring all our burdens to Him. He tells us that His yoke is easy and His burden is light (see Matthew 11:28–30). This shows a picture of us sharing a yoke with Him. A yoke is what a team of oxen would be tied to in order to pull a cart or plow. He is telling us that sharing a yoke with Him will make our burdens less because He will carry the weight for us.

We also see that it is listening to Him as well. If only one person is doing all the talking, it's not a conversation, but a testimony. Knowing that and being able to listen when He does try to tell us something is key. We must make sure we are not so busy talking that we miss out on what He is trying to tell us. We must be sure to stay in tune with Him and make sure that we are paying attention when He talks to us. Communication is a two-way street in our earthly relationships. We want our earthly partners to listen and talk with us. That is also the case in our heavenly relationship with Christ. We need to be sure that we are listening as much, if not more, than we are talking. Communication is a two-way street in our heavenly relationship, as well. If we will just be willing to pay attention, be patient, and listen, there is no telling what He may want to tell us next.

Chapter 4

Reading His Messages

The third way in which we can build a relationship with Christ is by reading our messages from Him. In our earthly relationships, we are never far from being able to receive any messages our significant other may send us. I do not know of anyone who, if their partner sent them a text, email, or letter, would not read that message within minutes of receiving it. We would never dream of saying, "I'll read it later. I'm busy right now"; no, you would read it immediately. We live in a day and time when you would want to know what they had to say to you, or see if something was wrong. In reality, Christ's message to us has been written down for us, and it is found in a handy little book, the Bible. Yet many of us never open the pages to read this message outside of a church service or a time of great need.

The Bible is Christ's love letter to us. It tells us about Him from beginning to end. You cannot read a book of the Bible and not find Him in it somehow. There was a song out several years ago sung by Aaron Jeffery called "He Is." It uses each book of the Bible to tell who or what Jesus is in each of the books of the Bible. It is a wonderful way to see that Jesus is involved and working through every book of the Bible, not just in the four Gospels. We can see Him active and moving in every single book. We see Him time after time not only in the New Testament, but in the Old Testament, as well. From the very beginning, we see Jesus there. In Genesis 1:26, God says, "Let Us make man in *our* image" (emphasis mine), we see that Jesus has been there since before time began. In John 1:1, John says, "In the beginning was the Word, and the Word was with God, and the Word was God." We also see the pre-incarnate Christ several times in the Old Testament. For example, in the book of Joshua we see Him in His pre-incarnate state as the Angel of the Lord, speaking to Joshua before the battle of Jericho. He is present throughout the entire book.

In the New Testament, we see Christ come to earth as the God-Man, and we see His life, ministry, death, and resurrection. Then we continue to see the creation of His Church (His Bride) throughout the rest of the New Testament, until we come to the end and see Him coming back as our Prince of Peace, our Bridegroom, to take us home and defeat Satan once and for all. Whew, that will make you shout right there! It is exciting to see that He was at work throughout the whole of time and not just for a small window of His thirty-three years spent on earth. Just as Hebrews 13:8 says, He was, is, and will forever be our unchanging Lord.

Our message from Him has been written down for ages, and it is very easily accessible to us. All we have to do is open it up and read it. Now, with modern-day technology, we have the Bible at our fingertips more than ever. We can have a physical book, or we can even have it as an app on our phones or tablets. We have the ability to carry His Word with us at all times. We have greater access to it than ever before, but I fear we study it less than ever before. We spend time on other apps watching videos and laughing, rather than spending time with our Fiancé and finding out more about Him. Just as reading someone's journal or diary would give you great insight into that person, so will reading and studying the Bible give you great insight into Christ as a Person.

As you read and study His Word, you will gain a better understanding of Him and how He wants us to live our lives and pursue His will for our lives. Imagine if we were given a handbook on our earthly relationships and were told that if we would read it we would be able to understand them completely and know them more intimately than ever before. I think I would want to spend a great deal of time in that book. This is what the Bible is. God has given us Himself in written form. I heard it explained one time like this: the Bible is God on paper. *Wow!* Just let that sink in for a moment—it is God on paper. The God of the universe is on paper, where you can read it. It's truly an incredible thought!

We are so blessed in our country and the time in which we live. As I stated before, we have access to the Bible in so many forms. It is simply amazing the ways we have to access it in this day and time. You can read it yourself or even have someone else read it to you. We have audio Bibles that you can listen to while you are doing your work. I even saw the other day, you can have Mufasa, the Lion King himself, James Earl Jones, read it to you on a new audio Bible! We have unprecedented access to the Word now. Back in the Middle Ages, the Bible was only available in Latin. The common man was not able to read, nor own a Bible of his own. It was many years before the Bible was translated into languages that common people could understand. There were some translations out there. The King James Bible really was the first time the Bible was openly available to the common man, but even then, very few were able to read it, as few commoners could read at all. Even in our time, people who live in other nations do not have as much access as we do to a Bible and have the privilege of reading it every day. For instance, people in India are still waiting for the Bible to be translated into all their languages. When one of them gets a Bible, it is as if they have been given a piece of gold, it is so precious to them. We here in America have lost that sense of preciousness about His Word. We have it readily available to us in so many ways that we have become used to the idea that there is a Bible in every store. Most of us have several Bibles in our homes. We need to get back to seeing His Word as precious.

As I stated before, John 1:1, 14 tells us, "The Word was with God, and the Word was God . . . the Word became flesh." That Word is Christ Jesus, our heavenly Fiancé, and if He is the Word, shouldn't we want to read that word and get to know Him better and better each day? You know, on earth we marry "till death do us part," but in heaven, we will be marrying for eternity, and I believe we should be building that heavenly relationship even more than we build our earthly one. This earthly relationship will end one day, either by their death or yours, but once we place our hand in those nail-scarred hands, we will *never* be out of His sight for all eternity.

We are all guilty of letting our busy lives get in the way of studying His Word. We all have so many things going on. Now that I am entering the empty-nest stage of life, I seem to have more time on my hands than before, but I remember all too well those days of juggling job, school, dinner, bath time, the kids' bedtime, and then getting to fall into bed myself, just to get up and do it all over again. Just thinking about it now makes me exhausted. I did well just to make enough time to kiss my husband some days—not to mention all the responsibilities we had with extracurricular activities for our children and at church. I wasn't just busy because of my being a pastor's wife, but we all are trying our best to do God's work in our churches. We are all trying to teach classes, help with Bible school, do mission outreach, and sing in the choir, among other things. There are so many things to pull at us every day, and we can just be exhausted by the time we fall into bed at night.

It may seem impossible to carve out that special quiet time with the Lord during these extremely busy times in which we live. But it is crucial to our growth as a Christian to do so. You cannot possible get to know Jesus more if you never read His Word or His message to you. I personally am a night owl, so the concept of getting up early to have that quiet time just does not work for me. So once the house is quiet and I am in bed, I pull my tablet out and spend just a few moments alone with Him before I close my eyes. Of course, if you can get up early in the morning before the chaos hits the floor, that is great, as well. It does not have to be an hour-long Bible study; it can be as simple as reading a chapter a day and having some prayer time. My husband likes to say in his sermons, "A chapter a day will keep the devil away." There is a lot of truth in that statement. If you get a lunch break at work and can spent few moments in reading the Word, then that works, as well. I find that lunch is a great time for me to do this. My husband is at work, the house is quiet, and I am able to concentrate on just me and Jesus having some time alone.

We can also learn so much more about Him through a deeper and closer study of the Bible. The personal one-on-one time spent with Him every day is where we get that relationship started, but when we do an in-depth Bible study, we are digging deeper into the meat of the information. We are getting more than just the top brushstroke of the information; we are getting down into the layers of what is there. It is through this type of study that we grow closer to Him and learn more about His true nature. This is how we grow to love Him more. When we really take time to dig into the little nuggets that are in His Word, we can grow so much more in our walk with Christ and learn about His true nature. This is why getting involved in a church or a ladies' group is so important to our growth in Christ. When we study with others, we can discover things we may have never noticed before. Someone in the group may read a verse and get a totally different meaning or nugget from it than you do, and in turn, you may be able to show them something different, as well. In-depth Bible study is important to the spiritual growth in our lives. The deeper we look into His Word, the more we will learn what His will is for our lives and what He has planned for us.

In the previous chapters, we related going to church as going on a date, if you will, with Jesus. Well, let's think about reading the Bible in that context. One-on-one time with Christ is like spending a one-on-one date with Him. Then, having a Bible study with fellow believers is like going on a group date. You are all getting to know each other better and learning about each other together. You can share experiences with each other and help each other see things that possibly you never thought about or noticed on your own. I have gathered so much knowledge and love for other ladies in these Bible studies. You grow to love the Bride of Christ together. After all, we will be spending quite a bit of time with the other members of the Bride of Christ in the future, so we had better learn to like some of them!

I would suggest to you that if you are not actively involved in a church or Bible study with other believers, you find one to get involved with. Spending time with other believers or members of the Bride of Christ is so very important to our growth in Christ. We learn from each other, and we are there for each other. I have said so many times over the years, that I do not know what people do who do not have a church family when they encounter troubled times. Yes, there are issues in church families, but are there not issues in our regular families, as well? You can always find a crazy cousin or two out there, and church families have crazy cousins, too. You just love them through it just like you would in your own family. We are looking at this from a relationship point of view, and just think of those troubled souls as the in-laws of the group. We have to be nice to them on holidays, and then we can go our separate ways. Believe you me, the good absolutely will outweigh the bad. As a pastor's wife, I have plenty of stories about church members, believe you me, but they are still our brothers and sisters in Christ. We are called to love them and fellowship with other believers.

So, as we close on looking at this point, we can see that we need to be actively involved in His Word, reading, studying, doing anything we can to help build this relationship, whether that is one-on-one time with Christ in our personal reading time or in a group setting diving deep into those Scriptures to see what nuggets of gold we can dig out together. We need to be actively learning more about His Word every day of our lives. Jesus is so interesting if you will take the time to get to know Him. We should want and yearn to know more about Him. When you really sit and think about it, we have a very small window of time here on earth compared to eternity. We have a small amount of time to learn about Jesus and how He loves us. Learn about His personality and His sense of humor. Yes, He does have one—have you seen ever a giraffe? Learn about how He does things and what He thinks about certain topics. We might be surprised at the things we learn and how it shapes the way we think about things and situations in the future. At one time, there were certain bracelets and other merchandise everywhere that said "WWJD"—do you remember those? What Would Jesus Do? Well, if you never study His Word to find out, how are you going to know what Jesus would do?

When we look at our earthly relationships, we see that we are always reading the messages our loved ones send to us. We make sure that we read a text as soon as it's sent. I would dare to say, most text messages are read within minutes of them being sent. Jesus sent us His messages two thousand years ago—He's just waiting for you to read them. We need to see that even more so now we need to be reading and studying the messages He has sent for us. We all can see that the time of His return is getting closer and closer. Our Bridegroom will be coming for us very soon, and we want to be sure that we have read His messages before He gets here. We need to be sure and set aside that time each day for us to read what message He has for us that day. If we do that, there is no telling what we can achieve and learn about Him. And when that day finally does come and we get to meet our heavenly Fiancé face-to-face, we will be the happiest bride in the world, because we will know exactly who we are marrying.

Chapter 5

Getting to Know All About Him

So, in conclusion, we can see that if we will work on these aspects of our Christian life, we will find ourselves so much closer to Christ than ever before. If we will spend time with Him, communicate with Him, and read His messages, then we will be able to grow the relationship we desire with Him and that He desires with us. Christ yearns for a close and personal relationship with us. His Spirit cries out within us to have that relationship with Him.

Imagine a man who cries out to be close to you, who wants to hear all your complaints and problems, and then in return who only asks that you love Him above everything else. He will never abandon you nor hurt you in any way. He only wants the absolute best for you. He came here and gave His life for the chance to be with you. Yet all He asks in return from you is that you love Him and live your life getting to know Him better. He knows that the more you get to know Him, the more you will love Him. Jesus is love, so there is no way to know Him and not love Him. The more we grow in understanding Him and what He wants for our lives, the more we will love Him. That is just simply the way it works.

Let us think about it in terms of being in a Fiancé relationship for just a moment again. Understand that I am not trying to make this story any less than what it is—I am simply trying to put it in the context from which this book was written.

The Prince of a nation leaves behind His throne and perfect Kingdom, where He has no problems or worries, to travel to a foreign land. While He is in this land, He lives as a peasant. He is laughed at, made fun of, and told He does not belong by His own neighbors with whom He grew up. He is constantly scrutinized for what He does and what He says by the religious people of the day. He has no home to call His own—He basically goes from place to place staying with friends. He has a group of friends who hang out with Him and are extremely loyal to Him, but they do not really understand what His mission is all about. Then finally, after all this, He is betrayed by one of His closest friends and arrested for a crime He did not commit. The whole kingdom cries out for Him to be executed. He is then taken and beaten until He is unrecognizable. A crown of thorns is put upon His head. He is spit on, and His beard is pulled out. Then finally, He is hung on a cross until He dies. Yet He is raised on the third day back to life. He does all of this only because He loves you and wants the opportunity to marry you.

We have heard stories about princes in our time who have renounced their thrones in order to marry whom they wanted. This is always painted as such a romantic gesture, a modern-day Romeo and Juliet, if you will. That a man would give up all he has to marry the love of his life, it seems unbelievable to us. But Jesus did that and more. He was the Prince of Glory, and yet He gave all that up to come here and do all that He did for you and me. Maybe if we put the story more into a romantic fairy-tale setting, it will ring more true to us. There is, nor will there ever be, a greater love story than that of Jesus Christ and His Bride. Jesus left the realms of glory for His Bride, He gave His life for His Bride, and one day very, very soon, He is coming back for His Bride.

We live in a time, as I stated in the previous chapter, when Jesus coming for His Bride is seeming very near. We are running out of time to get to know our Bridegroom. If you cannot look around at the times in which we live and see this, then you need to look harder. The Bible says in 2 Timothy 3:1–5 that the days will be as the days of Noah, when men will be lovers of themselves. If we are not at those days now, I shudder to think of them getting worse. We are in the days when we need to be preparing ourselves for His return. His Bride needs to be making herself ready.

We do that by the principles I have stated in this book: by spending time with Him, communicating with Him, and reading His messages. Those are the three things we must do to learn more about our Bridegroom and cultivate that relationship with Him so that when He does come for us, we will be excited to see Him. It really boils down to just doing two things: praying and reading/studying the Bible. It is really that simple. If we will pray and read the Word on a daily basis, the relationship will build itself. Jesus does all the hard work. All we have to do is make time for Him. Compared to what He has done for us, for Him to only ask of us a little bit of our time and love is not a great thing to ask. We should be daily on our knees thanking Him for what He has done for us. The fact that He wants a personal relationship with us is just mind-blowing. The God of the universe wants to talk to you on a daily basis, and that just blows the mind. You are His greatest treasure and the love of His life. Just let that sink in for a few moments. It is truly awe-inspiring and will make you want to put Him in the place He deserves—first place in your life.

It is my hope and prayer that after reading this book, you will see and desire a much closer walk with your Prince Charming, that you will see how much He truly loves you and what kind of relationship He desires to have with you. He truly does want to have a personal relationship with you. He truly does want to know all about you and have you know all about Him. In Psalm 17:8, the psalmist wrote that we are the "apple of Your eye; hide me under the shadow of Your wings." We are the apple of His eye, and He protects us just as a mother bird protects her young with her wings. That is how Jesus protects us. What an awesome picture of love that is. He takes care of us and protects us. He is our Advocate when Satan tries to accuse us of all the things we do wrong. Jesus stands up and says, "Leave her alone, she's Mine!" What a wonderful thing to know and experience in our lives.

I hope that you will use these three steps, spending time, communicating, and reading messages, to foster your relationship with Him. As I stated before, no one is going to love you more than Christ will. No one is going to do more for you than Christ can. No one is going to give you the best in life the way Christ will. And one day, when the eastern sky bursts open and our Prince Charming comes for us on His white horse to take us to His castle in the sky, away from all earthly worries and problems, we will be ready to meet Him with a greater understanding of who and what He is and a deeper love for Him. That will make us be ready and excited to marry our Prince Charming and live happily ever after with Him in His magnificent castle in the sky.

About the Author

Christa Griffin is a pastor's wife, mother, and teacher from Alabama. She has been married to her husband, Tim, for thirty-two years. Of those thirty-two years, she and her husband have spent twenty-six years in ministry, pastoring different churches in rural northwest Alabama. They have one daughter, Rachel, who got married five years ago and left her and Tim as empty-nesters. During their time in ministry, Christa has served in several areas, but she found that women's ministry is where her heart truly lies. She loves teaching other women about God and helping them grow closer to Him. She began teaching women's Bible studies and felt the idea for this book come to be. As an avid fan of fairy tales and princess stories, she began to notice a parallel in these stories to Jesus. It is her hope that women, young and old, will be able to forge a deeper relationship with Jesus through this book and begin to see the Lord Jesus as their coming Betrothed, the Prince of Peace.